Holidays

Chinese New Year

by Rebecca Pettiford

Bullfrog
Books

Ideas for Parents and Teachers

Bullfrog Books let children practice reading informational text at the earliest reading levels. Repetition, familiar words, and photo labels support early readers.

Before Reading

- Discuss the cover photo. What does it tell them?

- Look at the picture glossary together. Read and discuss the words.

Read the Book

- "Walk" through the book and look at the photos. Let the child ask questions. Point out the photo labels.

- Read the book to the child, or have him or her read independently.

After Reading

- Prompt the child to think more. Ask: Does your family celebrate Chinese New Year? What sorts of things do you see when it's the Chinese New Year?

Bullfrog Books are published by Jump!
5357 Penn Avenue South
Minneapolis, MN 55419
www.jumplibrary.com

Library of Congress Cataloging-in-Publication Data

Pettiford, Rebecca, author.
  Chinese New Year / by Rebecca Pettiford.
    pages cm. — (Holidays)
  "Bullfrog Books are published by Jump!."
  Summary: "This photo-illustrated book for beginning readers describes the holiday of Chinese New Year and the things people do to celebrate it. Includes picture glossary and index."
—Provided by publisher.
  Audience: Ages 5–8.
  Audience: K to grade 3.
  Includes bibliographical references and index.
  ISBN 978-1-62031-184-4 (hardcover: alk. paper) —
  ISBN 978-1-62496-271-4 (ebook)
  1. Chinese New Year—Juvenile literature.
[1. Holidays.] I. Title. II.
Series: Bullfrog books. Holidays.
  GT4905.P4625 2015
  394.261—dc23
                                          2014041409

Editor: Jenny Fretland VanVoorst
Series Designer: Ellen Huber
Book Designer: Michelle Sonnek
Photo Researcher: Michelle Sonnek

Photo Credits: All photos by Shutterstock except: age fotostock, 17; Alamy, 18–19, 22tr; Corbis, 9, 23tl, 24; iStock, 1, 4; Ngarto/Dreamstime, 8–9, 23br; SuperStock, 3, 5, 16, 22br, 23bl; Thinkstock, 6–7.

Printed in the United States of America at Corporate Graphics in North Mankato, Minnesota.

Table of Contents

What Is Chinese New Year?

Chinese New Year is a Chinese holiday.

Many people celebrate it.

Does it begin January 1?

No. It changes each year.

Each year is named
for an animal.

PIG

RAT

DOG

OX

ROOSTER

TIGER

MONKEY

RABBIT

GOAT

DRAGON

HORSE

SNAKE

What do we do
in the New Year?

We go to the temple.

We honor
our ancestors.

ancestors

Mom cleans the house.
We help her cook.

We put out a tray.

It has candy and nuts.

Red is a lucky color.

We put up
red lanterns.

Pretty!

Our family gives gifts.

Li gives PoPo oranges.

They are a symbol
of good luck.

Jin gets a red envelope.

What's inside? Money!

Let's go to the parade.
See the dragon?
It dances!

Wow! Fireworks!
Happy New Year!

Symbols of Chinese New Year

red lanterns

fireworks

oranges

red envelopes

Picture Glossary

ancestors
Members of a family who lived a long time ago.

PoPo
A name some Chinese children call their grandmother.

Chinese
Relating to the people, way of life, and language of China, a country in Asia.

symbol
An object that represents something else. In China, an orange is a symbol of good luck.

dragon
A symbol of wisdom in Chinese culture that is often linked to royalty.

temple
A building where people go to pray.

Index

To Learn More

Learning more is as easy as 1, 2, 3.

1) Go to www.factsurfer.com

2) Enter "Chinesenewyear" into the search box.

3) Click the "Surf" button to see a list of websites.

With factsurfer.com, finding more information is just a click away.